SuperStrata Quilts

Celebrating the Colors of Bali

PAMELA MOSTEK
and
SUSAN NELSEN

Martingale®
& COMPANY

SuperStrata Quilts:
Celebrating the Colors of Bali
© 2010 by Pamela Mostek and Susan Nelsen

That Patchwork Place® is an imprint of
Martingale & Company®.

Martingale & Company
20205 144th Ave. NE
Woodinville, WA 98072-8478 USA
www.martingale-pub.com

Credits

President & CEO: Tom Wierzbicki
Editor in Chief: Mary V. Green
Managing Editor: Tina Cook
Developmental Editor: Karen Costello Soltys
Technical Editor: Laurie Baker
Copy Editor: Marcy Heffernan
Design Director: Stan Green
Production Manager: Regina Girard
Illustrator: Adrienne Smitke
Cover & Text Designer: Stan Green
Photographer: Brent Kane
Travel Photography: Pamela Mostek and
                    Susan Nelsen

Printed in China
15 14 13 12 11 10   8 7 6 5 4 3 2 1

Library of Congress Cataloging-in-Publication Data is available upon request.

ISBN: 978-1-56477-988-5

Mission Statement

Dedicated to providing quality products and service to inspire creativity.

Acknowledgments

What a great adventure we had preparing for this book! Our trip to Bali was a delight, but that was the easy part of the process. Next came writing the book, which we had a great time doing. It was our first collaboration, and, naturally, there are those we need to thank for their help. Our thanks to:

Martingale & Company, for liking our idea of combining a super technique with a fabulous location. As always, working with them was a pleasure.

Our wonderful guide in Bali, Supy, for taking us to his temple festival and teaching us so much about the culture and people of his country, as well as his expertise at jumping out of the tour bus to direct traffic.

Mr. Ketut Swabawa, manager of the beautiful Komaneka at Bisma Hotel in Ubud, Bali, for his absolutely invaluable help in assisting us with the details of putting this book together. His generous nature is typical of all the people we met there.

Pak Tjok Agung Pemayan, for the opportunity to actually try the batiking process at his studio in the village of Pejing.

Those at the Pelangi Traditional Weaving Center in the village of Sideman, for welcoming us to watch their traditional ikat weaving process.

All the lovely citizens of Bali, who treated us with the utmost kindness and respect during our visit. Whether it was those who helped us at our hotels and restaurants or someone who answered our many tourist questions, every person we met was a joy.

Deb Roberts and her World of Quilts Travel, for arranging our trip to the beautiful island of Bali.

Pam would also like to thank:

As always, my husband, Bob, who proudly supports my artistic endeavors and understands when it seems that all I do is work. I couldn't do it without him, but I do wish he'd learn to cook too.

My machine quilter, Carol MacQuarrie, who has been adding her gorgeous finishing touch to my quilts for nine years. She's a true artist with her machine, and there is nothing ordinary about the stitching she adds to my quilts. But mostly I appreciate the pride she takes, the enthusiasm she shows, and the friendship we share.

Joan Vick, for her help in sewing several of the quilts in this book. With her expert piecing, I know my designs will be in good hands when I need a little extra help.

Beverly Holmes, for joining the team to be the official binding specialist. She does a great job of adding that very last step, and I am so appreciative of the time her help saves me.

My coauthor and dear friend, Susan, for being a perfect traveling companion and a red-hot technical editor.

Bernina of America, for providing me with my fabulous sewing machine. You may have heard it before, but it's true—nothing sews like a Bernina.

Susan would also like to thank:

First and foremost, my husband, Ken, who is ever so patient and always encouraging when it comes to my quilting dreams and adventures. He is my best supporter in all respects!

My son, Kyle, for all his computer expertise when my computer misbehaves. He always figures it out.

My two sisters, Loraine Manwaring and Peggy Hicks, for spending a weekend binding these quilts. Both of you are wonderful.

My friend and kindred spirit, Pam. Your enthusiasm and creativity inspire me.

Contents

BALI BOUND 10

MEET THE SUPERSTRATA 12

MAKING THE SUPERSTRATA 14

The Quilts

ROYAL THREADS 20

BALI BLUE SKY 28

BUTTERFLY DANCE 34

STANDING GUARD 42

MONKEY TAILS 50

MANGO MADNESS 58

FLOWER MARKET 64

GARDEN TROPICS 72

QUILTMAKING BASICS 77

MEET THE AUTHORS 80

Bali Bound

So, what is a SuperStrata, and how does it relate to beautiful Bali? They go together fabulously—the gorgeous scenes and sites of Bali together with a construction technique that sizzles; create the perfect recipe for a lovely-to-look-at and super-informative book.

But first the story. Pam was asked to teach on a textile tour to Bali, and, of course, she needed her trusty travel companion, Susan, to join the tour. Naturally, Susan enthusiastically agreed. We've shared great textile travels in the past and knew this would be another fantastic learning experience for fabric lovers like us—with lots of laughs and good times.

So we began thinking, researching, and learning a little about Bali to be prepared for what we'd find on this island far on the other side of the world. We knew it was famous for its gorgeous batiks that are hand printed and imported to the United States. But there's more. In our pre-trip exploration, we also discovered that Bali is world famous for its single- and double-ikat weaving. Ikat weaving uses a resist dying process in which the threads are tied together so that they don't absorb dye; this creates a pattern in the weaving. If just the warp or weft threads are dyed, it's referred to as single ikat and if both the warp and weft threads are dyed, it's double ikat. The more we read, the more excited we became. Textiles are hugely important in Bali culture and daily life. In fact, it seemed like Bali would be a true textile treasure trove!

Because both of us are veteran authors and quilt designers, when we discover a place with breathtaking beauty, intriguing culture, *and* wonderful textiles, the next thing that comes to mind is a book! Even before our trip, we'd discovered much to share and knew it would be a fabulous opportunity to bring our experience to life for quilters and textile lovers.

But what kind of a book? As enticing as the culture is, we decided to incorporate our textile travels with a technique we had used. We expanded it, perfected it, and named it SuperStrata (more about that in "Meet the SuperStrata" on page 12). We knew this technique would be a great way to show off the colors and culture of Bali, our inspiration.

Armed with our research, our book idea, our cameras, and our great expectations, we set out on our Bali adventure. Even with all this preplanning and pre-thinking, we were not prepared for the huge impact the experience would have upon us.

It was all there, just as we'd read about: the ancient temples and architecture, the frantic and vividly colored markets, the patchwork-quilt-like rice fields, the cool high-mountain views, the pristine beaches, the amazing textiles, and the bling of gold. But what touched our hearts the most was the people. We realize that's a pretty broad statement, but it's true. Their kind, gentle, and considerate ways and captivating smiles were things we hadn't anticipated. Memories of the wonderful people we met were most certainly a little piece of Bali that we brought home with us.

Oh yes, we also brought home lots and lots of fabrics. We even sacrificed clothing and shoes to make room in our suitcases for more fabric! In fact, the tour company had to send an extra truck to the hotel for our group's luggage for the return flight. After all, when you combine 25 fabric lovers with fabulous and inexpensive textiles, the result is definitely a mountain of luggage.

The quilts in *SuperStrata Quilts* were all inspired by the Balinese beauty and culture, and we'll share a little of that with you throughout this book, along with as many photos as we can squeeze in! We hope you'll be intrigued by our experiences and love the technique. We have thoroughly enjoyed putting this book together for you. In fact, we may even call it a labor of love in view of our truly memorable adventure.

We've already decided that we're going back. But that's another story!

Our best,
        ~Pam and Susan

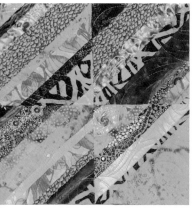
Diagonal SuperStrata

Straight SuperStrata

Curved SuperStrata

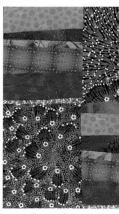
Slanted SuperStra

Meet the SuperStrata

Throughout this book, any time you sew strips of fabric together
along the long edges, you have created a SuperStrata. If you learned
to quilt when we did, you may remember this pieced fabric as a
strip set, but our term is SuperStrata.

Not only do we use many strips of fabric, we've taken the process a
step further and created not just straight SuperStrata, but
diagonal SuperStrata, curved SuperStrata, and slanted
SuperStrata. The result is a piece of unique fabric ready to turn
into colorful, scrappy-looking blocks or block elements.

4. Referring to the instructions for the quilt, use a see-through ruler and rotary cutter to cut the segments or blocks. Begin by squaring up the SuperStrata; then cut into segments and blocks according to the quilt instructions.

Diagonal SuperStrata

1. Referring to the project instructions for the length of the SuperStrata strips, follow steps 1–3 above to make a straight SuperStrata.

2. Follow the manufacturer's instructions to apply lightweight fusible interfacing to the wrong side of the SuperStrata. This will stabilize the fabrics so that you can easily cut diagonal

blocks on the bias without stretching the fabric out of shape.

3. Using a see-through ruler and a soft-lead pencil, mark the bias on the wrong side of the SuperStrata by aligning the 45°-angle line of the ruler along the bottom edge of your SuperStrata.

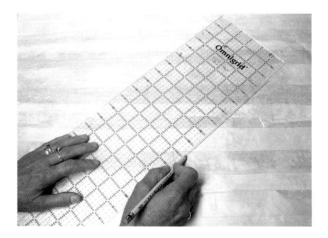

4. Using your see-through ruler as a guide, cut along the drawn line with your rotary cutter.

5. Following the angled line, cut the SuperStrata into strips the width given in the project instructions. Subcut the strips into blocks or segments.

Curved SuperStrata

1. Refer to the instructions for your quilt project for the strip dimensions and the number of strips required for your SuperStrata. Arrange the strips in the order you will use them.

2. Place the first fabric strip right side up on the cutting mat. Position the second fabric strip right side up and overlap it with the right edge of the first strip by 1".

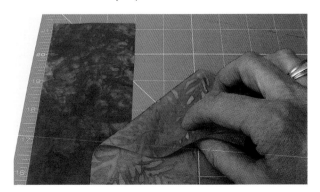

3. Align the left edge of a strip of 1"-wide blue painter's tape that is longer than the fabric strips with the left edge of fabric strip 2, covering the overlap area. Secure the ends of the tape to the cutting mat. The tape stabilizes the fabric strips for cutting and defines your cutting area.

4. With a rotary cutter, cut gentle curves through the taped area, working from edge to edge. The more gentle the curve, the easier it will be to stitch the seam. Making the cut straight at the beginning and ending of the curve will also make stitching the seam easier.

5. Gently lift the tape (still attached to fabric strip 2) to the *left* of the cut and discard. Move fabric strip 2 away from fabric strip 1, exposing a small cut strip of fabric strip 1. Discard this small strip as well. Gently remove the last strip of tape from the remaining fabric strip 2.

6. With right sides together and fabric strip 2 on top of fabric strip 1, pin the starting edges of the strips even with one pin. Using a ¼" seam allowance, sew the curved edges together. Gently maneuver the top strip to align the edges with the bottom strip as you stitch the curves of the seam. Do not try to pin this seam because you will need to adjust the fabric edge as you sew.

7. Press the piece from the right side using the tip of the steam iron along the seam to open the piece. Press the entire seam flat, and then turn the piece over to double-check that the entire seam allowance is pressed in the same direction.

8. Repeat steps 2–7 to add additional strips as needed for your project.

9. When you're finished adding strips, use a see-through ruler and rotary cutter to square up one end of the SuperStrata; then follow the project instructions for cutting the SuperStrata into blocks or segments.

Slanted SuperStrata

1. All the strips we cut for the slanted SuperStrata are 2½" x 21". The number of strips you need will depend on how you cut them at an angle after they're attached to another strip; the quilt instructions will give you an approximate number, although you may need to add more to complete your SuperStrata.

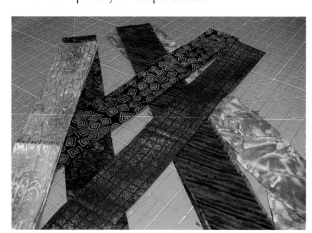

2. Using a rotary cutter and clear acrylic ruler, cut one side of the first strip at an angle.

3. Position the next strip so that its straight edge is even with the slanted edge of the last strip. Pin and sew together. Press the seam allowances flat from the wrong side, and then press in one direction from the right side.

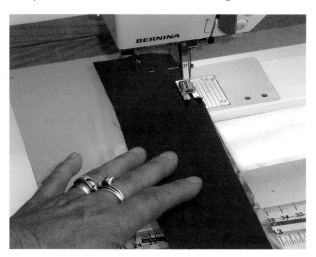

4. Next cut the second strip at a slant that is different from the first strip, giving variety and contrast in the SuperStrata.

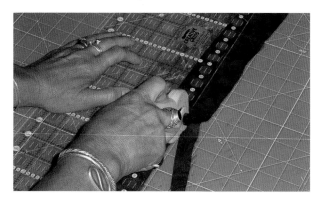

5. Continue to add additional strips by stitching, pressing, cutting, and sewing again. Press all seam allowances in the same direction as you pressed them in step 3. Continue until you have a SuperStrata the width needed for your project.

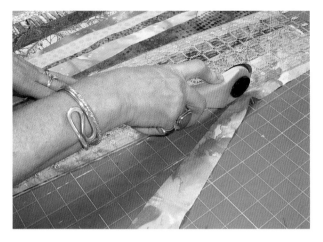

6. Square up one end of the SuperStrata, and then follow the project instructions to cut the SuperStrata into blocks or pieces to use in the quilt.

Save the Selvage

For most of us, the first thing we do when we're cutting fabric is trim off the selvage. Not so in Bali. Textile experts there told us that the selvage is very sacred, and to cut it off would allow the spirit to escape from the cloth. Their ceremonial garments are usually made from one long length of fabric, or sarongs, that are wrapped around their bodies and secured rather than cut. This way the spiritual nature of their fabric can be preserved.

Royal Threads

As we researched Balinese textiles before going to Bali, I was drawn to a photograph of a ceremoni songket (see "Songket" on page 26). When I got to Bali, I wanted to see some songkets firsthand. I was thrilled to watch a songket of purple and silver threads being woven at factory that we visited, and in the market I bought two songkets to bring home with me.

Fashioned after a traditional songket woven of red silk and metallic gold threads, this quilt is fit for royalty. Fortunately, you don't have to wait for a ceremonial occasion to use these royal threads. I used red and gold metallic fabrics to add glimmer and shine.

* Susan *

Finished quilt: 53½" x 72½"
Finished block: 10" x 10"

Materials

Yardage is based on 42"-wide fabric, unless otherwise noted.

4 yards *total* of assorted red fabrics for
    SuperStratas
3 yards of red-with-gold metallic print for
    SuperStratas, sashing, inner border, middle
    border, and binding
6 fat quarters of assorted yellow fabrics for blocks
1⅜ yards of fabric with gold metallic print for
    middle and outer borders
3¼ yards of fabric for backing
61" x 80" piece of batting
4½ yards of 22"-wide lightweight fusible
interfacing

Cut It Up

All measurements include ¼"-wide seam allowances.

From the red-with-gold metallic print, cut:
3 strips, 2" x 42"
7 strips, 1½" x 42"
7 strips, 2¼" x 42"

From the assorted red fabrics and the remaining red-with-gold metallic print, cut a *total* of:
130 strips in various widths between 1" and
    2" x 42"

From the assorted yellow fat quarters, cut a *total* of:
40 squares, 5⅞" x 5⅞"

From the fabric with gold metallic print, cut:
7 strips, 4" x 42"; crosscut into 28 rectangles,
    4" x 8½"
4 strips, 2½" x 42"
3 strips, 2" x 42"

Create the SuperStrata Pieces

1. Refer to "Diagonal SuperStrata" on page 15 to use the assorted red and red-with-gold strips of various widths to make a SuperStrata section at least 30" wide. I used about 38 strips to make my SuperStrata, but you may

use more or less. Repeat to make a total of two SuperStratas.

2. With the interfacing fused to each SuperStrata, cut 5⅞"-wide diagonal strips. Crosscut the strips into 40 squares, 5⅞" x 5⅞".

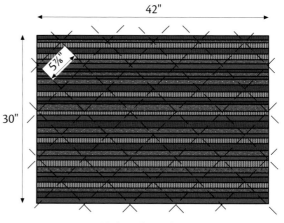

Make 2 SuperStratas.
Cut 40 squares.

3. Refer to "Straight SuperStrata" on page 14 to sew enough of the remaining assorted red and red-with-gold strips of various widths together to make a SuperStrata section at least 9" wide. I used about 10 strips to make mine, but yours may vary. Repeat to make a total of four SuperStratas. Trim each SuperStrata to 8½" wide. Crosscut the SuperStratas into 14 segments 7½" wide and 14 segments 2½" wide.

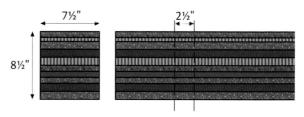

Make 4 SuperStratas.
Cut 14 segments, 7½" wide,
and 14 segments, 2½" wide.

Make the Pinwheel Blocks and Rows

1. Using a soft-lead pencil and a see-through ruler, draw a diagonal line from corner to corner on the wrong side of each yellow 5⅞" square.

by Susan Nelsen

2. With right sides together, pair a yellow square with a diagonal SuperStrata square. The drawn line on the yellow square must be going in the opposite direction of the seams on the SuperStrata square. Stitch ¼" from *each* side of the drawn line. Cut on the drawn line and press. Repeat to make a total of 80 units. Each pair of squares will yield two units. Trim the extended corners.

Make 80.

3. Arrange the triangle squares as shown to make 10 each of Pinwheel block A and Pinwheel block B. Press the seam allowances in the directions indicated.

Pinwheel block A.
Make 10.

Pinwheel block B.
Make 10.

4. Join five A blocks side by side to make row A. Repeat to make a total of two rows. Press the seam allowances in one direction. Join five B blocks side by side to make row B. Repeat to make a total of two rows. Press.

Row A.
Make 2.

Row B.
Make 2.

Make the Songket Blocks and Rows

1. Using a soft-lead pencil and a see-through ruler, draw a diagonal line from corner to corner as shown on the wrong side of 14 gold metallic print 4" x 8½" rectangles for piece C. Draw a diagonal line from corner to corner in the opposite direction on the remaining 14 gold metallic print rectangles for piece D.

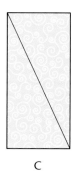 

C   D

2. On the right side of a straight SuperStrata 7½" x 8½" segment, mark the center of one 7½" side at the edge of the fabric. Then make a mark ¼" to the left and ¼" to the right of the center dot.

Center
¼"   ¼"

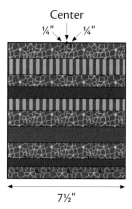

7½"

3. With right sides together, position a gold metallic print C piece on a marked SuperStrata segment from step 2 so that the diagonal line aligns with the bottom-left corner of the SuperStrata and the mark that is to the right of the center mark at the top edge. You may want to secure this with a pin at each corner. Stitch on the diagonal line. Press the gold metallic print to the right side along the seam line. Position a gold metallic print D piece on the segment in the opposite direction as shown,

aligning the diagonal line with the bottom-right corner and the mark that is to the left of the center mark at the top edge; stitch and press as before. Once you have both gold print pieces sewn to the SuperStrata and you know that the upper gold corners match the SuperStrata corners, trim the excess gold metallic print even with the sides of the SuperStrata segment. Repeat to make a total of 14 Songket blocks.

Songket block.
Make 14.

4. Join seven Songket blocks side by side as shown. Repeat to make a total of two rows. Sew the three red-with-gold 2" x 42" strips together end to end to make one long strip. From the pieced strip, cut two strips, 2" x 49½". Add these strips to the bottom of each block row. Press.

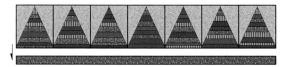

Make 2.

Put It Together

1. Sew the red-with-gold 1½" x 42" strips together end to end to make one long strip. From the pieced strip, cut five sashing strips, 1½" x 50½".

2. Refer to the quilt assembly diagram at right to lay out the Pinwheel block and the sashing strips in vertical rows. Sew the rows and sashing together. Press.

3. Sew the SuperStrata 2½" x 8½" segments together end to end to make two pieced border strips, 2½" x 50½", trimming as necessary. Sew these borders to the sides of the quilt center. Press.

4. Add the Songket block rows to the top and bottom of the quilt center, with the red-with-gold strip toward the quilt center. Press.

5. Refer to "Adding Borders" on page 77 to add the outer borders using the gold metallic print 2½"-wide strips for the side borders and the gold metallic print 2"-wide strips for the top and bottom borders.

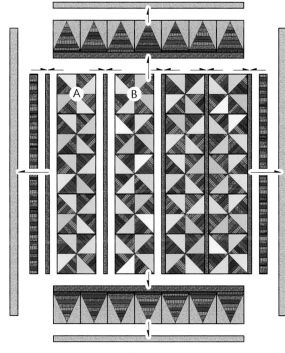

Quilt assembly

Finish It Up

Refer to "Quiltmaking Basics" on page 77 for specific instructions regarding each of the following steps.

1. Layer the quilt top, batting, and backing, unless you plan to take your quilt to a long-arm quilter. Hand or machine quilt as desired. I machine quilted the center with lots of loops in an open design, and then stippled the gold outer borders.

2. Use the red-with-gold 2¼"-wide strips to bind the quilt.

Songket

Songket cloth, which has been made for centuries, is a gorgeous textile shimmering with gold or silver threads that is worn for a grand occasion and can symbolize status and wealth among the Balinese. Often a brilliant red highlighted with sparkling metallic gold or silver, the songket is definitely not an everyday textile in the Balinese culture. Of course, in Western cultures such as ours, festive dressing can also be part of a celebration, but the difference is in how we use our special textiles. We would undoubtedly create a party outfit by selecting a pattern (or making up our own), cutting it out, sewing it together, and perhaps embellishing it with sparkling beads or threads or whatever strikes our fancy. Not so in Bali. Instead of cutting and sewing, they use their songket in a very different way. It isn't sewn together, but multiple layers of printed and woven songket are instead wrapped, draped, and tied around the body in a very artful fashion. With its rich history and gorgeous glitz, songket cloth is the ultimate Balinese celebration outfit!

Mirrored Mountains

I brought all but one of these fabrics home from Bali and had a great time using them in this quilt. It differs from the songket quilt in the way that I set the SuperStrata patches. Instead of the Pinwheel design, I arranged the SuperStrata units as flying geese, working from the center out in each row. If you play with the same patches in a given quilt, you can come up with numerous creative ways to arrange them. I also cut the SuperStrata strips narrower for my blocks, varying from ¾" to 1½" wide. Rather than one color family of fabrics for the SuperStratas, I used strips from 80 different fabrics in a wide range of colors and values! Strikingly different, yet the basic block construction is the same in both quilts.

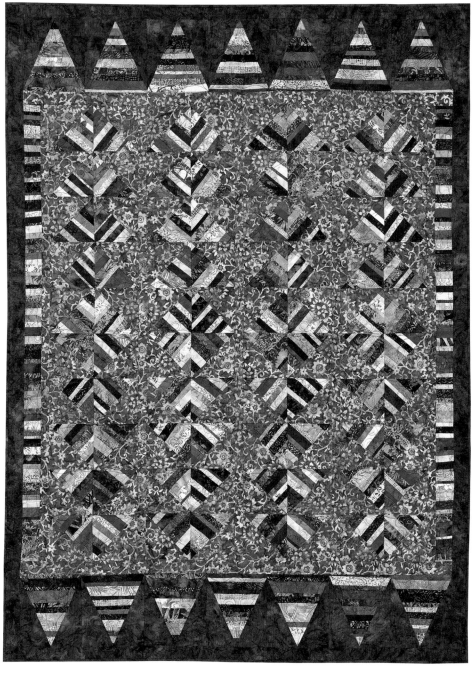

by Susan Nelsen, 53½" x 72½"

Bali Blue Sky

I'll always remember the glorious blue skies of Bali, especially at the point where the blue of the sky met the deep bluish green of the ocean. To capture that look, I created this quilt in a multitude of shades of green and blue prints with even a little purple thrown in. Diagonal SuperStrata blocks come together to create the diamond shapes in this beautiful blue sky quilt.

* Pam *

Finished quilt: 48" x 48"
Finished block: 6" x 6"

Materials

Yardage is based on 42"-wide fabric.

4 yards *total* of assorted blue, turquoise, purple, and green fabrics for SuperStratas and pieced outer border
½ yard of green fabric for inner border and corner triangles
⅓ yard of dark blue fabric for middle border
½ yard of fabric for binding
3 yards of fabric for backing
56" x 56" piece of batting
3½ yards of 22"-wide lightweight fusible interfacing

Cut It Up

All measurements include ¼"-wide seam allowances.

From the assorted blue, turquoise, purple, and green fabrics, cut a *total* of:
12 strips, 2½" x 42"
70 strips in various widths between ¾" and 2" x 42"

From the green fabric for inner border and corner triangles, cut:
1 strip, 5½" x 42"; crosscut into 4 squares, 5½" x 5½"
4 strips, 1½" x 42"

From the dark blue fabric, cut:
5 strips, 1½" x 42"

From the binding fabric, cut:
6 strips, 2¼" x 42"

Create the SuperStrata Blocks

1. Refer to "Diagonal SuperStrata" on page 15 to use the assorted blue, turquoise, purple, and green strips of various widths to make a SuperStrata section at least 30" wide. I used about 33 strips to make my SuperStrata, but you may use more or less. Repeat to make a total of two SuperStratas.

2. With the interfacing fused to each SuperStrata, cut 6½"-wide diagonal strips. Crosscut the strips into 36 blocks, 6½" x 6½".

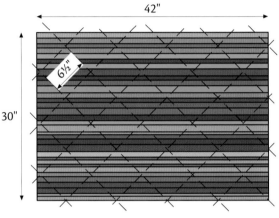

Make 2 SuperStratas.
Cut 36 blocks.

3. Using a soft-lead pencil and a see-through ruler, draw a diagonal line on the wrong side of the green 5½" squares. Position a 5½" square on a 6½" SuperStrata block as shown. Notice the direction of the SuperStrata seams. Stitch on the line, trim the seam allowances to ¼", and press. Repeat to make a total of four corner blocks.

Make 4.

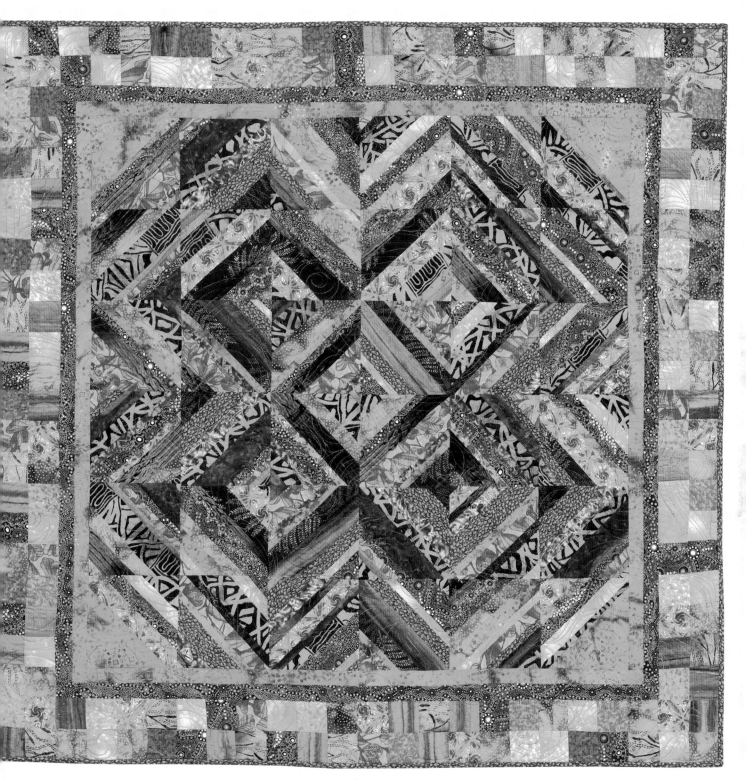

by Pamela Mostek

Make the Pieced Outer-Border Strips

1. With the assorted blue, turquoise, purple, and green 2½" x 42" strips, make a straight SuperStrata using two strips. Repeat to make a total of six SuperStratas. Crosscut the SuperStratas into 88 segments, 2½" wide.

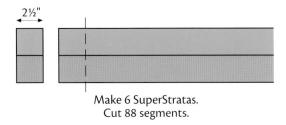

2½"

Make 6 SuperStratas.
Cut 88 segments.

2. Join 20 segments side by side to make a side border. Repeat to make a total of two side borders. In the same manner, make top and bottom borders with 24 segments each.

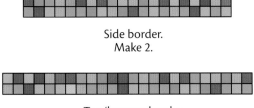

Side border.
Make 2.

Top/bottom border.
Make 2.

Put It Together

1. Refer to the quilt assembly diagram at right to arrange the 32 SuperStrata blocks and the four corner blocks into six rows of six blocks each. Note the direction of the SuperStratas in each block. As you arrange the blocks, the diamond pattern will emerge in the quilt center. Sew the blocks in each row together. Press the seam allowances in opposite directions from row to row. Sew the rows together.

2. Refer to "Adding Borders" on page 77 to add the inner border using the green 1½"-wide strips. Repeat to add the middle border using the dark blue 1½"-wide strips.

3. Sew the pieced side borders to the sides of the quilt top, and then add the pieced top and bottom border strips.

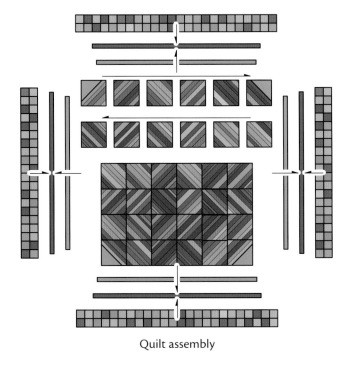

Quilt assembly

Finish It Up

Refer to "Quiltmaking Basics" on page 77 for specific instructions regarding each of the following steps.

1. Layer the quilt top, batting, and backing, unless you plan to take your quilt to a long-arm quilter. Hand or machine quilt as desired. I had this machine quilted in an overall pattern.

2. Use the 2¼"-wide binding strips to bind the quilt.

Celebration!

A flurry of fabrics and colors come together in this lively version of "Bali Blue Sky." Rather than using a narrow palette of similar shades, for "Celebration!" I used as many different colors and prints as I could put together. The combination reminds me of one of my favorite things about the Balinese: the way they mix their colors and patterns without regard to matching and coordinating—by our standards, a very fearless use of color.

by Pamela Mostek, 48" x 48"

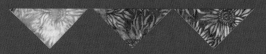

Butterfly
Dance

We learned so much about the culture
and traditions of Bali from our guide, Supy.
According to him, butterflies symbolize
men and flowers symbolize women. The
Bali culture is rich with stories told through
music and dance, so I'll take the liberty to
tell a story with my Bali batik quilt—these
bright butterflies are courting the fragrant
flowers in this glorious garden.

* Susan *

Finished quilt: 50½" x 60½"
Finished block: 10" x 10"

Materials

Yardage is based on 42"-wide fabric, unless otherwise noted.

3⅛ yards of multicolored floral batik for background
6 fat quarters or 1½ yards *total* of assorted solid or almost solid batiks for SuperStratas
⅞ yard of gold batik for border and binding
⅓ yard of yellow batik for border
3¼ yards of fabric for backing
59" x 69" piece of batting

Cut It Up

All measurements include ¼"-wide seam allowances.

From the assorted solid or almost solid batiks, cut a *total* of:
60 strips, 1½" x 14"

From the multicolored floral batik, cut:
3 strips, 10½" x 42"; crosscut into:
    1 rectangle, 10½" x 15½"
    6 squares, 10½" x 10½"
10 strips, 5½" x 42"; crosscut into:
    3 rectangles, 5½" x 15½"
    6 rectangles, 5½" x 10½"
    40 rectangles, 3" x 5½"
    24 squares, 5½" x 5½"
3 strips, 4½" x 42"; crosscut into 24 squares, 4½" x 4½"

From the gold batik, cut:
4 strips, 3" x 42"; crosscut into 48 squares, 3" x 3"
6 strips, 2¼" x 42"

From the yellow batik, cut:
3 strips, 3" x 42"; crosscut into 36 squares, 3" x 3"

Create the SuperStrata Butterfly Blocks

1. Referring to "Straight SuperStrata" on page 14, randomly select five assorted batik 1½" x 14" strips and sew them together to make a SuperStratas. Repeat to make a total of 12 SuperStratas. Crosscut *each* SuperStrata into two squares, 5½" x 5½" (24 total). Keep the matching squares together.

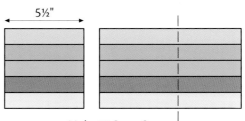

Make 12 SuperStratas.
Cut 2 segments from each (24 total).

2. Using a soft-lead pencil and a see-through ruler, draw a diagonal line from corner to corner on the wrong side of each floral batik 4½" square. With right sides together, position marked squares on a pair of SuperStrata squares as shown. Notice the direction and order of the SuperStrata strips and the direction of the diagonal lines for each pair. Stitch on the drawn lines. Trim ¼" from the stitching lines and press. Repeat for each pair of SuperStrata squares.

Make 12 pairs.

by Susan Nelsen

3. Arrange a pair of squares from step 2 and two floral 5½" squares in two horizontal rows. Sew the pieces in each row together. Press. Sew the rows together to create a Butterfly block. Press. Repeat to make a total of 12 blocks.

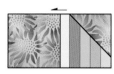
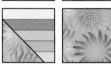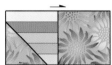

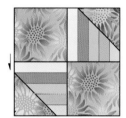

Make 12.

Make the Flying-Geese Border Strips

1. Draw a diagonal line from corner to corner on the wrong side of each yellow 3" square and 44 of the gold 3" squares.

2. With right sides together, position a yellow 3" square on a floral batik 3" x 5½" rectangle as shown. Stitch on the marked line. Trim ¼" from the stitching line. Press. Repeat on the opposite end of the rectangle. Repeat to make a total of 18 yellow flying-geese units.

Make 18.

3. Repeat step 2 using the marked gold 3" squares and the remaining floral batik 3" x 5½" rectangles to make 22 gold flying-geese units.

Make 22.

4. To make the side border strips, alternately stitch six gold flying-geese units and five yellow flying-geese units side by side. Repeat to make a total of two border strips.

Make 2.

5. To make the top and bottom border strips, alternately stitch five gold flying-geese units and four yellow flying-geese units side by side. Add a gold 3" square to each end. Repeat to make a total of two border strips.

Make 2.

Put It Together

Because of the variety in the colors of the butterflies, you'll want to use a design wall to preview the placement of the blocks. Refer to the quilt assembly diagram on page 39 to help you preview the quilt, and then follow the row-by-row construction steps.

1. For vertical row 1, arrange three Butterfly blocks, two floral batik 10½" squares, and one floral batik 5½" x 10½" rectangle. Sew the pieces together and press.

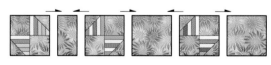

Row 1

2. For vertical row 2, arrange three Butterfly blocks, two floral batik 10½" squares, and one floral batik 5½" x 10½" rectangle. Sew the pieces together and press.

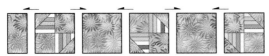

Row 2

3. Sew a floral batik 5½" x 10½" rectangle to four Butterfly blocks as shown.

Make 2 of each.

4. For vertical row 3, arrange the four units from step 3 and the three floral batik 5½" x 15½" rectangles. Sew the pieces together and press.

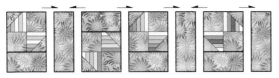

Row 3

5. For vertical row 4, arrange two Butterfly blocks, two floral batik 10½" squares, and the floral batik 10½" x 15½" rectangle. Sew the pieces together and press.

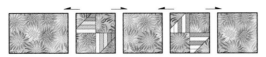

Row 4

6. Sew the rows together and press. Add the side borders to the sides of the quilt top and press. Join the top and bottom borders to the quilt top. Press.

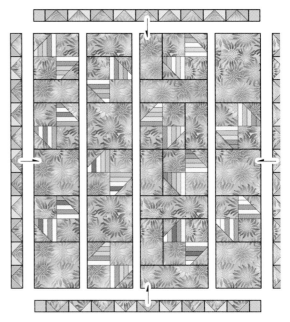

Quilt assembly

Finish It Up

Refer to "Quiltmaking Basics" on page 77 for specific instructions regarding each of the following steps.

1. Layer the quilt top, batting, and backing, unless you plan to take your quilt to a long-arm quilter. Hand or machine quilt as desired. I used black thread to stitch a design on the butterfly wings and in the outer border. Using cream thread, I quilted a body with antenna for each butterfly. Through the floral background I quilted a meandering stitch, adding more flowers and some dragonflies for interest.

2. Use the gold print 2¼"-wide strips to bind the quilt.

Moonlight Flight

Made using the same pattern as "Butterfly Dance," this quilt utilizes a contemporary and graphic floral fabric with a striking black background to give the butterflies a moonlight garden to explore. For the butterflies, I used a deliberate arrangement of strips to make the SuperStrata so that each butterfly was made with a variety of prints in the same color.

by Susan Nelsen, 50½" x 60½"

Balinese Dancers

Photo courtesy of Komaneka at Bisma

The Balinese dancers were breathtakingly beautiful to watch. Their graceful hands and mysterious eyes, elaborate make-up and glitzy costumes were all part of the magic. It was almost hypnotic to watch them as they performed for their audience. But, it's not just the professionals who dance in Bali. Beginning at a very early age, everyone learns to dance. It's part of their temple and cultural festivals and celebrations throughout the year and throughout their lives. Watching the beautiful Balinese dancers was a total tourist treat.

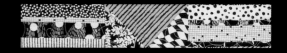

Standing Guard

I love the drama of black-and-white fabrics, and to the Balinese, this color combination is very meaningful (see "Black-and-White Poleng" on page 48). As a tribute to their black-and-white checked fabric, I used a lively combination of black-and-white prints to create this bed-sized quilt. And for a little extra pizzazz, I added a touch of yellow, which is a symbol of purity in Bali.

* Pam *

Finished quilt: 80½" x 96½"
Finished block: 11¼" x 11¼"

Materials

Yardage is based on 42"-wide fabric.

8 yards *total* of assorted black-and-white prints
     for SuperStratas and side and corner setting
     triangles
1⅜ yards of black-and-white-with-yellow print for
     top and bottom borders
⅞ yard of yellow print for blocks
¾ yard of fabric for binding
7¼ yards of fabric for backing
89" x 105" piece of batting

Cut It Up

All measurements include ¼"-wide seam allowances.

**From the assorted black-and-white prints,
cut a *total* of:**

4 squares, 17¾" x 17¾"; cut into quarters
     diagonally to yield 16 side setting triangles
2 squares, 9" x 9"; cut in half diagonally to yield 4
     corner setting triangles
62 squares, 6½" x 6½"; cut in half diagonally to
     yield 124 triangles
100 strips in various widths from ¾" to 2" x 42"

From the yellow print, cut:

4 strips, 6½" x 42"; crosscut into 20 squares. Cut
     each square in half diagonally to yield 40
     triangles.

From the black-and-white-with-yellow print, cut:
5 strips, 8½" x 42"

From the binding fabric, cut:
10 strips, 2¼" x 42"

Create the SuperStrata Segments

Refer to "Straight SuperStrata" on page 14 to use
the assorted black-and-white strips of various
widths to make a SuperStrata section at least 9"
wide. Repeat to make a total of 11 SuperStratas.
I used from six to nine strips to make each
SuperStrata, but you may use more or less. Trim
each SuperStrata to 8½" wide. Crosscut the
SuperStrata into 41 squares, 8½" x 8½".

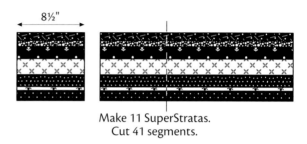

Make 11 SuperStratas.
Cut 41 segments.

Make the Blocks

1. To make block A, sew black-and-white print
    6½" triangles to opposite sides of a SuperStrata
    square as shown. Press. Sew black-and-white
    6½" triangles to the remaining two sides of
    the square. Press. Repeat to make a total of 17
    blocks.

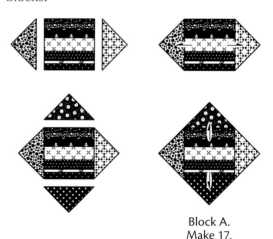

Block A.
Make 17.

by Pamela Mostek

2. Repeat step 1 using the remaining SuperStrata squares, black-and-white 6½" triangles, and yellow triangles to make blocks B–G in the color combinations shown. Note the direction of the SuperStrata when adding the triangles.

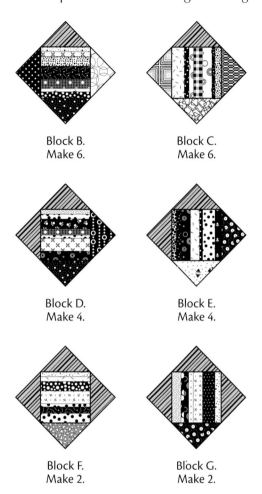

Block B.
Make 6.

Block C.
Make 6.

Block D.
Make 4.

Block E.
Make 4.

Block F.
Make 2.

Block G.
Make 2.

Put It Together

1. Refer to the quilt assembly diagram at right to lay out the blocks in diagonal rows, following the direction of each SuperStrata center. Add the side setting triangles; these are cut oversized, but you will trim them later. When you're pleased with your arrangement, sew each diagonal row together. Press the seam allowances in opposite directions from row to row. Join the rows, adding the corner triangles last. Trim the outside edges ¼" from the block points.

2. Refer to "Adding Borders" on page 77 to add the top and bottom borders to the quilt.

Quilt assembly

Finish It Up

Refer to "Quiltmaking Basics" on page 77 for specific instructions regarding each of the following steps.

1. Layer the quilt top, batting, and backing, unless you plan to take your quilt to a long-arm quilter. I quilted this in an overall pattern because in the busy collection of prints, the quilting tends to visually disappear.

2. Use the 2¼"-wide binding strips to bind the quilt.

Batik Beauty

Yes, it's the same design—but with a totally different look. Rather than using an active mix of fabrics like in "Standing Guard," in this smaller version I used a simple palette of batiks created by hand in Bali and exported to the United States. Luckily for us, we can find similar hand-dyed batiks in our local quilt shops. The solid-looking batik pieces are a great place to show off your machine quilting using a metallic thread for a little Bali bling.

by Pamela Mostek, 54" x 54"

Black-and-White Poleng

This simple black-and-white checked fabric is a popular pattern in the United States, and we seemed to see it everywhere in Bali. At the entrance to a temple we saw it adorning the stone guardians at the doorway. It was draped at the hundreds, even thousands, of small temple offerings found throughout Bali. It's so much a part of the culture, we easily became accustomed to its dramatic presence.

Called poleng, we learned that it is not an elegant celebration cloth like the songket (see page 26) but is a simply woven or printed black-and-white cloth. Its significance comes not from the fabric itself but the opposite colors of black and white. To the Balinese, it symbolizes all the opposites of the world that make up the whole of life—night and day, dry and rainy seasons, mountain and sea, and good and evil. It conveys a special message of the complexity of life to the people of Bali that they understand but rarely verbalize.

Monkey Tails

I'm used to seeing squirrels running through a park, not monkeys, but there they were. Monkeys roamed the forest and hid in the trees in some of the areas of Bali that we visited. They were pretty good pickpockets too, if they thought you might have a snack hidden away. Can you see the monkey tails in this quilt?

* Susan *

Finished quilt: 52½" x 52½"
Finished blocks: 6" x 12" and 6" x 6"

Materials

Yardage is based on 42"-wide fabric, unless otherwise noted.

6 fat quarters of coordinating blue fabrics for SuperStratas (4 different prints, 1 duplicate print, and 1 striped fabric)

5 fat quarters of coordinating yellow fabrics for SuperStratas (4 different prints and 1 striped fabric)

5 fat quarters of coordinating pink fabrics for SuperStratas (4 different prints and 1 striped fabric)

5 fat quarters of coordinating green fabrics for SuperStratas (4 different prints and 1 striped fabric)

5 fat quarters of coordinating purple fabrics for SuperStratas (4 different prints and 1 striped fabric)

½ yard of fabric for binding

3⅜ yards of fabric for backing

61" x 61" piece of batting

1½ yards of 22"-wide lightweight fusible interfacing

Cut It Up

All measurements include ¼"-wide seam allowances.

From *each* of the 4 different blue fat quarters and the striped fat quarter, cut:
4 strips, 3" x 18" (20 total)
3 strips, 2½" x 18" (15 total)

From the duplicate blue fat quarter, cut:
4 strips, 2½" x 18"

From *each* of the yellow, pink, green, and purple fat quarters, cut:
4 strips, 3" x 18" (80 total)
3 strips, 2½" x 18" (60 total)

From the binding fabric, cut:
6 strips, 2¼" x 42"

Create the Curved SuperStrata Blocks

1. Using the blue 3" x 18" strips, make four groups of five different prints each. Refer to "Curved SuperStrata" on page 16 to make a curved

SuperStrata from each group. Be sure to vary the order of the strips in each.

2. Cut one 6½" x 12½" segment from each of two blue SuperStrata as shown for the A blocks.

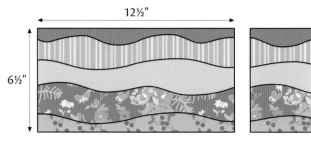

Block A.
Cut 1 rectangle from each
of 2 SuperStratas (2 total).

3. From another blue SuperStrata, cut two 6½" squares as shown for the B blocks.

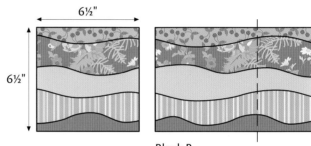

Block B.
Cut 2 squares from 1 SuperStrata.

4. Before cutting the final blue SuperStrata, refer to step 2 of "Diagonal SuperStrata" on page 15 to add interfacing to the SuperStrata. Then cut two 6½" squares on *an angle* from this SuperStrata as shown for the C blocks. (The width of this SuperStrata does not allow for a complete 45° angle for cutting these squares, so maximize the angle to cut these.)

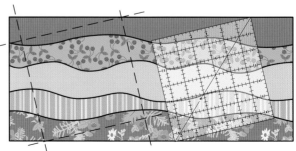

Block C.
Cut 2 tilted squares, 6½" x 6½",
at a maximized angle.

by Susan Nelsen

5. Repeat steps 1–4 to make and cut the curved SuperStrata using the yellow, pink, green, and purple 3" x 18" strips. You'll have 10 A blocks, 10 B blocks, and 10 C blocks. Set these aside for now.

Create the Straight SuperStrata Blocks

1. Refer to "Straight SuperStrata" on page 14 to use three different blue 2½" x 18" strips to make a SuperStrata. Repeat to make a total of five SuperStratas. Crosscut into nine segments, 6½" wide.

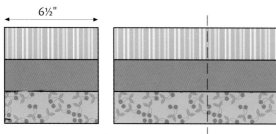

6½"

Make 5 SuperStratas.
Cut 9 segments.

2. Repeat step 1 with the yellow, pink, green, and purple 2½" x 18" strips to make the number of SuperStratas shown. Crosscut into the number of segments indicated. Set aside the remaining strips for the outer border.

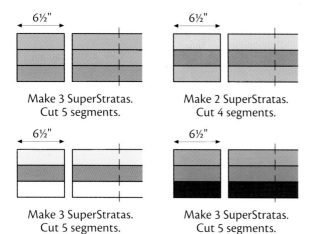

6½"

Make 3 SuperStratas.
Cut 5 segments.

6½"

Make 2 SuperStratas.
Cut 4 segments.

6½"

Make 3 SuperStratas.
Cut 5 segments.

6½"

Make 3 SuperStratas.
Cut 5 segments.

Put It Together

1. Using a design wall and referring to the quilt assembly diagram at right as a reference only, arrange the A, B, and C curved SuperStrata blocks into rows for the quilt center. Sew A, B, and C blocks together to make a unit, and then arrange three units in each of the three rows. You will not use all of the curved SuperStrata blocks.

2. When you're pleased with your arrangement, sew the units in each row together, and then sew the rows together. Press.

3. For the inner border, arrange the straight SuperStrata blocks around the quilt center, alternating the direction of each block. You will need six blocks for each side and eight blocks for the top and bottom. Once you like *your* arrangement, sew the blocks together for each side border, and then sew these borders to the quilt center. Join the blocks in the top and bottom borders, and then add them to the quilt. Press.

4. For the outer border, cut the remaining 2½" x 18" strips into 2½" x 6½" rectangles as follows: eight purple, seven blue, seven yellow, five green, and five pink. Also cut one 2½" square *each* of blue, yellow, pink, and green. Arrange the rectangles around the quilt center, adding a square at each corner. You will need eight rectangles *each* for the side and top and bottom borders. Sew the rectangles together for each side border, and then sew the borders to the sides of the quilt. Sew the rectangles for the top and bottom rows together, adding the squares at each end. Sew these borders to the top and bottom of the quilt. See the quilt assembly diagram, top right.

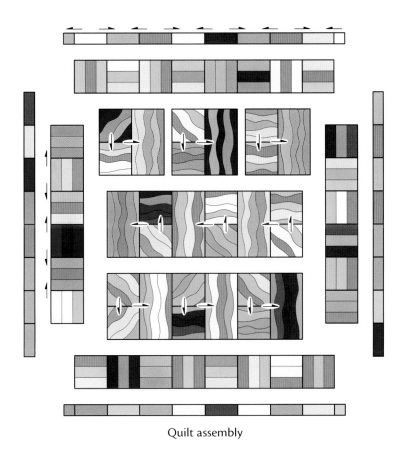

Quilt assembly

Finish It Up

Refer to "Quiltmaking Basics" on page 77 for specific instructions regarding each of the following steps.

1. Layer the quilt top, batting, and backing, unless you plan to take your quilt to a long-arm quilter. Hand or machine quilt as desired. I machine quilted a gently curving line across the center of the quilt, and then echoed the curves and added some swirls as I worked my way to the edges of the quilt. The quilting lines are ¾" apart.

2. Use the 2¼"-wide binding strips to bind the quilt.

The Newspaper

It's the old joke—what's black and white and read all over? The newspaper! Instead of five colors, I used an all-time favorite combination of black, white, and red. Even in Bali, the black-and-white fabric of the Bali polengs was often paired with a red fabric. I used only 6" SuperStrata curved blocks in the center, surrounded by a ring of straight SuperStrata blocks, and finished it off with a solid border rather than a pieced border. It's amazing how different a quilt can look with a change in the colors!

by Susan Nelsen, 48" x 48"

Monkeys Galore

Yes, that's right, monkeys. We visited an amazing forest in Bali that is home to an abundance of monkeys. Not only that, there's also a shopping street in the city of Ubud that is appropriately called Monkey Forest Road, where the monkeys lounge on the sidewalks, amble into the open-air shops, and stroll across the road into the nearby wooded area. No one seems to pay much attention to them.

Neither of us are what you might call avid monkey lovers, but we had to admit they were almost charming in spite of our slight misgivings. OK, they were actually pretty cute. One thing to remember should you ever go to Bali—don't eat, or even look like you might eat, around them or they will climb right up your leg and try to get the goodies out of your hand!

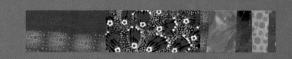

Mango Madness

Super delicious . . . that's the only way to describe the fabulous fruit concoctions we enjoyed in Bali. In fact, our mango smoothies became one of the favorite parts of every day, especially the hot days. Served in a tall glass, their color was (almost) as delightful as their taste. I captured the delicious orange color in these fabrics, and named this quilt in honor of our favorite taste treat, the mango smoothie. We were absolutely mad about them!

* Pam *

Finished quilt: 54½" x 68½"
Finished block: 6" x 8"

Materials

Yardage is based on 42"-wide fabric.

5 yards *total* of assorted orange, red, and rust
   fabrics for SuperStratas and borders
1½ yards of coordinating dark fabric for alternate
   blocks and third border
⅝ yard of fabric for binding
3⅓ yards of fabric for backing
63" x 77" piece of batting

Cut It Up

All measurements include ¼"-wide seam allowances.

**From the assorted orange, red, and rust fabrics,
cut a *total* of:**
50 strips, 2½" x 42"; crosscut into 100 strips,
   2½" x 21"
12 strips, 1½" x 42"; crosscut into various lengths
   from 6" to 15"

**From *each* of the remainder of 4 different
orange, red, and rust fabrics, cut:**
2 strips, 2½" x 42" (8 total)

From the coordinating dark fabric, cut:
7 strips, 6½" x 42"; crosscut into 25 rectangles,
   6½" x 8½"
1 strip, 2½" x 42"; crosscut into 6 rectangles,
   2½" x 6½"

From the binding fabric, cut:
7 strips, 2¼" x 42"

Create the SuperStrata Pieces

1. For the horizontal SuperStrata blocks, refer to
   "Slanted SuperStrata" on page 18 to use the
   2½" x 21" strips to make a SuperStrata section
   at least 9" wide. Repeat to make a total of

four SuperStratas. Trim each SuperStrata to
8½" wide. Crosscut the SuperStratas into 10
segments, 6½" wide.

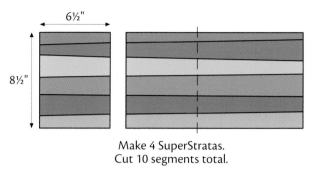

Make 4 SuperStratas.
Cut 10 segments total.

2. For the vertical SuperStrata blocks, refer to
   "Slanted SuperStrata" to use the 2½" x 21"
   strips to make a SuperStrata section at least
   7" wide. Repeat to make a total of seven
   SuperStratas. Trim each SuperStrata to 6½"
   wide. Crosscut the SuperStratas into 14
   segments, 8½" wide.

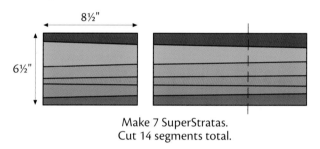

Make 7 SuperStratas.
Cut 14 segments total.

3. For the SuperStrata border, refer to "Slanted
   SuperStrata" to use the 2½" x 21" strips to
   make a SuperStrata section at least 13" wide.
   Repeat to make a total of two SuperStratas.
   Trim the SuperStratas to 12½" wide. Crosscut
   the SuperStratas into 14 segments, 2½" wide.

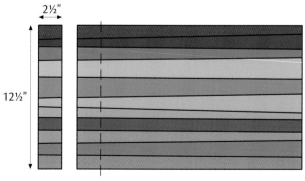

Make 2 SuperStratas.
Cut 14 segments total.

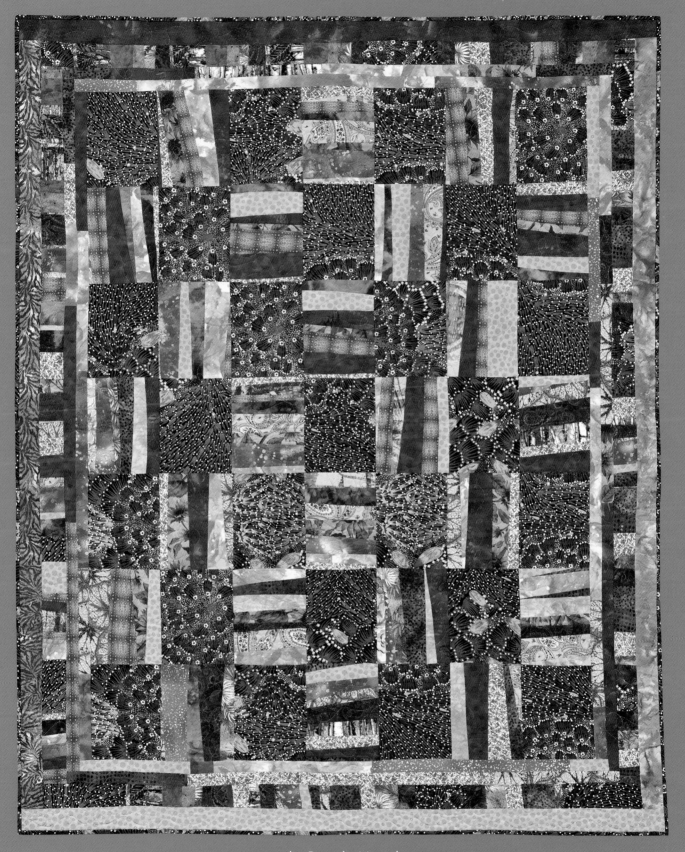

by Pamela Mostek

Put It Together

1. Refer to the quilt assembly diagram below to arrange the SuperStrata blocks and the coordinating dark print 6½" x 8½" alternate blocks into seven rows of seven blocks each, alternating the blocks in each row and from row to row. Sew the blocks in each row together. Press the seam allowances toward the alternate blocks. Sew the rows together. Press.

2. For the first border, sew the orange, red, and rust 1½"-wide strips together to equal at least 210". Refer to "Adding Borders" on page 77 to add the border to the quilt center.

3. For the second border, repeat step 2 with more of the 1½"-wide strips, making the pieced strip at least 220" long.

4. Refer to "Adding Borders" to use the SuperStrata 2½" x 12½" segments and the coordinating dark print 2½" x 6½" rectangles to make pieced strips for the third border and add them to the quilt top. Refer to the quilt photo to see how the segments and strips are randomly put together to make this border.

5. For the outer border, sew each pair of red, orange, or rust 2½" x 42" strips together to make four pieced strips. Using one pieced strip for each side of the quilt, add the borders to the quilt top in the same manner as the previous borders.

Finish It Up

Refer to "Quiltmaking Basics" on page 77 for specific instructions regarding each of the following steps.

1. Layer the quilt top, batting, and backing, unless you plan to take your quilt to a long-arm quilter. Hand or machine quilt as desired. I machine quilted this with a small overall pattern using a metallic thread for some added pizzazz.

2. Use the 2¼"-wide strips to bind the quilt.

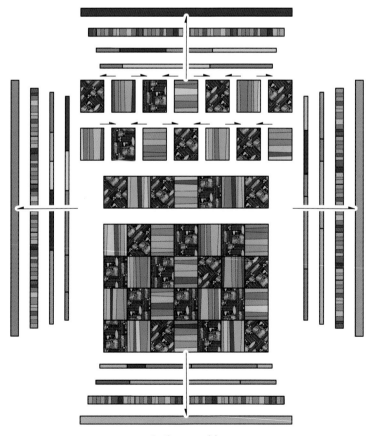

Quilt assembly

Phoenix Rising

This graceful bird, the phoenix, is a popular motif found on the printed sarongs of Bali. To make this smaller, more traditional-looking version of Mango Madness, I used a green phoenix-print sarong for the alternate blocks and border, and then added the multicolored SuperStrata blocks. The glitter of gold is so much a part of the culture of Bali that I made it part of my quilt too.

by Pamela Mostek, 45" x 54"

Flower Market

Shopping in the open air markets of Bali was an amazing experience, unlike anything I've ever done. The hordes of people, the cramped vendor booths, the variety of wares, and the noise of so much hustle and bustle is hard to describe, but I tried to capture the rich and brilliant colors of the flower vendor in this quilt. Can you see the individual booths all nestled together to create the flower market? It's time to barter!

— * Susan *

Finished quilt: 56" x 73"
Finished block: 12" x 12"

Materials

Yardage is based on 42"-wide fabric, unless otherwise noted.

3 yards of red print for block centers, setting triangles, and binding

10 fat quarters of assorted blue, green, and purple prints for SuperStratas

3 fat quarters or ¾ yard *total* of assorted gold and orange prints for SuperStratas

3½ yards of fabric for backing

64" x 81" piece of batting

Cut It Up

All measurements include ¼"-wide seam allowances.

From the fat quarters of assorted blue, green, and purple prints, cut a *total* of:

45 strips, 3" x 21"

From the fat quarters of gold and orange prints, cut a *total* of:

14 strips, 2½" x 21"

From the red print, cut:

3 squares, 22¼" x 22¼"; cut into quarters diagonally to yield 12 side setting triangles (you will use 10)

2 squares, 13¾" x 13¾"; cut in half diagonally to yield 4 corner setting triangles

18 rectangles, 4½" x 6½"

7 strips, 2¼" x 42"

Create the SuperStrata Segments

1. Arrange the blue, green, and purple print strips into nine groups of five strips *each*, varying the strips from group to group. Refer to "Straight SuperStrata" on page 14 to sew the strips in each group into a SuperStrata. After pressing,

trim each SuperStrata to 12½" wide, trimming an equal amount from each side. Crosscut the SuperStratas into 36 segments, 4½" wide.

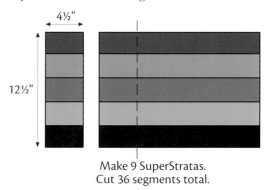

Make 9 SuperStratas.
Cut 36 segments total.

2. Arrange the gold and orange print strips into pairs, varying the prints from pair to pair, to make seven straight SuperStratas. Crosscut the SuperStratas into 36 segments, 3½" wide.

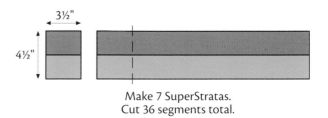

Make 7 SuperStratas.
Cut 36 segments total.

Make the Flower Market Blocks

1. Sew a gold/orange SuperStrata segment to each short side of a red print 4½" x 6½" rectangle. Press the seam allowances toward the rectangle. Repeat to make a total of 18 units.

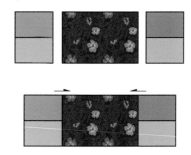

Make 18.

flower market

by Susan Nelsen

2. Sew a blue/green/purple SuperStrata segment to each long side of a unit from step 1. Press the seam allowances toward the center. Repeat to make a total of 18 blocks.

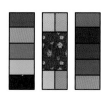

Make 18.

Put It Together

1. Sew a red print side setting triangle to each side of a Flower Market block as shown. Press. Trim the triangles even with the top of the block. Repeat to make a total of two rows.

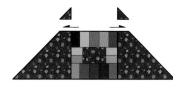

Make 2.

2. Sew three blocks together, rotating them as shown, and then add a red print side setting triangle to each end of the row. Press. Trim the triangles even with the top of the blocks. Repeat to make a total of two rows.

 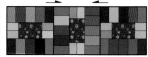 

Make 2.

3. Sew five blocks together, rotating them as shown. Add a red print side setting triangle to the left end of the row. Press. Trim the triangle even with the top of the blocks. Repeat to make a total of two rows.

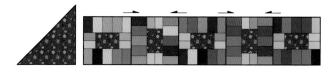

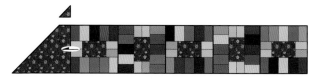

Make 2.

4. Join the two rows from step 3 and trim the extended corner of the triangles even with the sides of the rows.

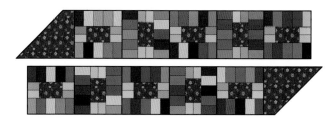

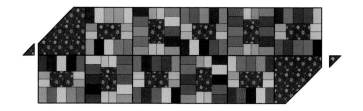

5. Refer to the quilt assembly diagram to arrange the rows. Sew the rows together. Trim the extended corners of the side setting triangles, and then add the corner setting triangles.

Quilt assembly

Finish It Up

Refer to "Quiltmaking Basics" on page 77 for specific instructions regarding each of the following steps.

1. Layer the quilt top, batting, and backing, unless you plan to take your quilt to a long-arm quilter. Hand or machine quilt as desired. I machine quilted a small overall design on all the red print areas in the blocks and outside borders, and then used wavy serpentine lines on all the SuperStratas.

2. Use the red print 2¼"-wide strips to bind the quilt.

Ocean Sunset

Using the same quilt pattern, the fabric choice here is a little more subtle and calm, with the outside border a soft bluish green. Half the blocks are made with red, orange, and gold Super-Stratas with a bluish green center. The other half of the blocks are made with red centers and blue, green, and gold SuperStratas. The blocks are then alternated throughout the quilt center. This is a soothing mix, reminiscent of an ocean sunset in Bali.

by Susan Nelsen, 56" x 73"

Local Markets

One of our favorite travel activities is visiting local markets. The markets in Bali are certainly at the top of our market list! The amazing colors, flowers, produce, people, noise, and of course the textiles were all incomparable.

Flowers of vivid colors were sold in baskets, and the produce was absolutely irresistible—even if we weren't quite sure what it was! The gorgeous colors everywhere put us in designer overload, but we soaked it all up and took lots of photos.

Then there were the textiles. Booth after booth of fabulous fabrics—cottons, rayons, and silks of all colors and prints—all created in Bali. To say they were amazing is simply a huge understatement. And the prices were wonderful for our tourist budgets. Truly the textile booths were one of the most memorable parts of our trip, so naturally we came home with stacks of textile souvenirs!

Garden Tropics

Being a color lover, I particularly enjoyed the lively way the Balinese mixed colors and patterns in their clothing and design. Prints of all sizes and colors were mixed and matched with delightful results. I used the same approach to create the diagonal SuperStratas for this quilt. The more colors and patterns the better, in the true Balinese way!

* Pam *

Finished quilt: 59½" x 78⅝"
Finished block: 4" x 4"

Materials

Yardage is based on 42"-wide fabric.

3 yards *total* of assorted green fabrics for
     SuperStratas and plain blocks
2½ yards *total* of assorted pink fabrics for
     SuperStratas and plain blocks
1⅝ yards of green print for setting triangles and
     border
⅝ yard of fabric for binding
3½ yards of fabric for backing
62" x 79" piece of batting
4 yards of 22"-wide lightweight fusible interfacing

Cut It Up

All measurements include ¼"-wide seam allowances.

From the assorted green fabrics, cut a *total* of:
52 squares, 4½" x 4½"
80 strips in various widths from ¾" to
     2" wide x 21"

From the assorted pink fabrics, cut a *total* of:
32 squares, 4½" x 4½"
80 strips in various widths from ¾" to
     2" wide x 21"

From the green print, cut:
2 strips, 7" x 42"; crosscut into 9 squares, 7" x 7".
     Cut each square into quarters diagonally to
     yield 36 side setting triangles (you will use 34).
2 squares, 3¾" x 3¾"; cut in half diagonally to
     yield 4 corner setting triangles
7 strips, 4½" x 42"

From the binding fabric, cut:
7 strips, 2¼" x 42"

Create the SuperStrata Blocks

1. Refer to "Diagonal SuperStrata" on page 15
    to use the assorted green 21"-long strips of
    various widths to make a SuperStrata section
    at least 34" wide. I used about 40 strips to
    make my SuperStrata, but you may use more
    or less. Repeat to make a total of two green
    SuperStratas.

2. Repeat step 1 with the assorted pink 21"-long
    strips of various widths to make two pink
    SuperStratas.

3. With the interfacing fused to each pink and
    each green SuperStrata, cut 4½"-wide diagonal
    strips. Crosscut the strips into 46 green and 46
    pink blocks, 4½" x 4½".

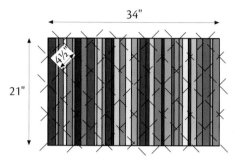

Make 2 green and 2 pink SuperStratas.
Cut 46 green and 46 pink blocks.

Put It Together

1. Using a design wall and referring to the quilt
    assembly diagram on page 76 as a reference
    for color placement, arrange the SuperStrata
    blocks and the assorted green print and pink
    print 4½" squares into diagonal rows.

    Have fun experimenting with your own
    scheme for placing the SuperStrata blocks and
    print squares into rows within each color area
    as shown in the assembly diagram. You may
    use more or fewer of each kind of block as
    you arrange the quilt on the design wall. You
    will have blocks left over. Add the side and
    corner setting triangles to the design wall to
    see the whole quilt center.

2. Sew the pieces in each diagonal row together.
    Press the seam allowances in opposite
    directions from row to row. As you complete
    each row, return it to the design wall to keep
    the rows in order. Once all the rows are
    complete, sew the rows together. Add the
    corner triangles last.

by Pamela Mostek

3. Refer to "Adding Borders" on page 77 to add the border using the green 4½"-wide strips.

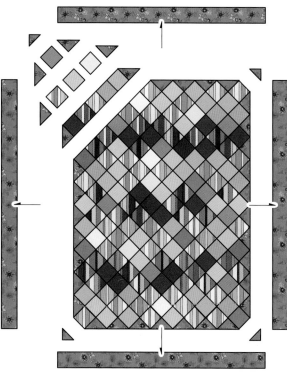

Quilt assembly

Finish It Up

Refer to "Quiltmaking Basics" on page 77 for specific instructions regarding each of the following steps.

1. Layer the quilt top, batting, and backing, unless you plan to take your quilt to a long-arm quilter. Hand or machine quilt as desired. I machine quilted this with a small overall pattern because of the many seams in the quilt top.

2. Use the 2¼"-wide binding strips to bind the quilt.

Another Thought

Bali Gold

Shopping the textile markets of Bali, we found many gorgeous sarongs that we could use for creating quilts, and we came home with a nice collection! I used a glitzy gold-and-dark-blue sarong for the solid blocks and even used the printed ends, which are sometimes different than the rest of the sarong, for borders. By arranging the SuperStrata and solid blocks in a slightly different pattern, I created an elegant but very different look than the livelier "Garden Tropics."

by Pamela Mostek, 51" x 51"

Quiltmaking Basics

This section includes helpful instructions for completing the projects in this book. Refer to it if you have questions about a specific technique. Of course, you may instead use your own favorite quiltmaking techniques. To make sure you're pleased with your finished quilt, always stitch accurate ¼"-wide seam allowances.

Adding Borders

1. Measure the length of the quilt top through the center. Cut two border strips to this measurement, piecing as necessary.

2. Mark the center of the quilt sides and the border strips. Pin the border strips to the sides of the quilt, matching the center marks and ends and easing as necessary. Sew the border strips in place and press the seam allowances toward the border.

3. Measure the width of the quilt top through the center, including the side border strips just added. Cut border strips to this measurement, piecing as necessary. Mark the centers, pin, and sew the border strips to the top and bottom of the quilt. Press the seam allowances toward the border.

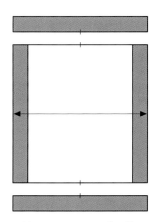

Measure center of quilt, side to side, including borders. Mark centers.

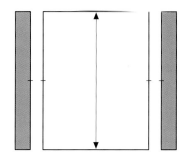

Measure center of quilt, top to bottom. Mark centers.

Pressing

Press carefully after each stitching step. This is especially important when making your SuperStrata. Press on the back, and then press again on the front, being careful not to stretch or pull the fabric with your iron.

Finishing Your Quilt

The following information will help you give your quilts an attractive, professional-looking finish.

LAYERING AND BASTING

If you're taking your quilt to a long-arm quilter, you don't need to layer and baste it. The following information pertains to quilting it yourself.

The quilt "sandwich" consists of the backing, batting, and quilt top. We recommend that you cut both the batting and the backing at least 6" larger than the quilt top on all sides. For large quilts, you will probably need to sew two or three lengths of fabric together to make a backing piece that is large enough. Remove the selvages before sewing and press the seam allowances open to reduce the bulk.

1. Spread the pressed backing, wrong side up, on a clean, flat surface and anchor it with pins or masking tape. Center the batting over the backing, smoothing out any wrinkles.

2. Center the pressed quilt top, right-side up, over the batting. Smooth out any wrinkles and make sure the edges of the quilt top are parallel to the edges of the backing.

3. For machine quilting, pin the layers together with safety pins. Begin pinning in the center and work toward the outside edges, placing

pins every 3" to 4" over the entire surface, or you may prefer to use one of the basting sprays that are on the market today.

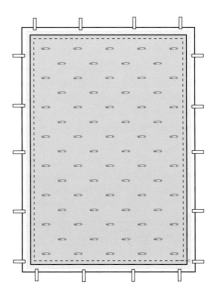

QUILTING

The quilts in this book were machine quilted, but you can choose your favorite quilting method to finish your project. Many quilters today have their quilts finished by talented professional quilters, but if you prefer to do your own machine quilting, check your local quilt shop for books, stencils, or even classes to get you started.

BINDINGS

To make straight-cut, double-layer (French) binding, begin by cutting 2¼"-wide strips across the fabric width. You'll need enough strips to go around the perimeter of the quilt, plus about 10" for seams and corners. The number of strips needed has already been calculated for the quilts in this book.

1. With right sides together, sew the strips together on the diagonal as shown to create one long strip. Trim the excess fabric and press the seam allowances open.

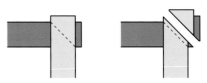

Joining straight-cut strips

2. Cut one end of the strip at a 45° angle and press it under ¼". Press the strip in half lengthwise, wrong sides together.

Fold line

3. Begin stitching about 3" from the folded end of the binding strip. Using a ¼"-wide seam allowance, stitch the binding to the quilt, keeping the raw edges even with the quilt-top edge. End the stitching ¼" from the corner of the quilt and backstitch.

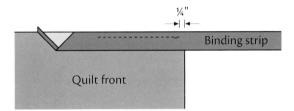

¼"

Binding strip

Quilt front

4. Fold the binding up, away from the quilt, and then back down onto itself, aligning the raw edges with the quilt edge. Begin stitching at the edge, backstitching to secure, and end ¼" from the lower edge. Repeat the folding and stitching process on the remaining corners.

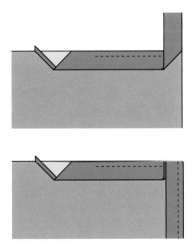

5. When you reach the beginning of the binding, lap the strip over the beginning stitches by about 1" and cut away any excess binding, trimming the end at a 45° angle. Tuck the end of the binding into the fold and complete the seam.

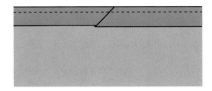

6. Fold the binding to the back. Blindstitch the binding in place, including the miter that forms at each corner.

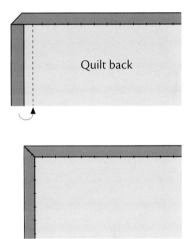

Quilt back

Meet the Authors

Susan and Pam

Even though *SuperStrata Quilts* is the first book they've written together, both Pam and Susan are veterans at authoring creative books for the quilting world. In addition, both of them are involved in a variety of other professional quilting activities.

Pam is a nine-time Martingale & Company author who also designs quilts and other projects for her design and publishing company, Making Lemonade Designs. She puts her love of color to work as a fabric designer and teaches both traditional- and art-quilting classes throughout the country. Her original art quilts have been included in a number of national shows and exhibits.

Susan is the owner and designer of Rasmatazz Designs, her quilt-design and publishing company. She has authored two previous quilt books for Martingale & Company and has self-published three others. She is a freelance technical editor in the quilt-book publishing world. In case this isn't enough to keep her days full, she's an active long-arm machine quilter, quilting all of her own quilts plus those for others as well.

Pam lives in Cheney, Washington, with her husband, Bob, while Susan lives in Idaho Falls, Idaho, with her husband, Ken. Both are involved mothers and grandmothers who always find time to squeeze family into their busy schedules.

There's More Online

• Go to Susan Nelsen's www.rasmatazzdesigns.com to find patterns, peruse a quilt gallery, and sign up for the Rasmatazz newsletter.

• Visit www.pamelamostek.com to see quilts, read Pam's blog, find patterns, and more.